JOY OF MISSING OUT

JOY OF MISSING OUT

Ana
Božičević

BIRDS, LLC | MINNEAPOLIS, NEW YORK, RALEIGH

Birds, LLC
Minneapolis, New York, Raleigh
www.birdsllc.com

Cover designed by Eric Amling
Interior designed by Michael Newton
Cover art by Eric Amling

Library of Congress Cataloging-in-Publication Data: Božičević, Ana
Joy Of Missing Out/Ana Božičević
Library of Congress Control Number: 2017931086

First Edition, 2017
ISBN-13: 978-0-9914298-7-5
Printed in the United States of America

JOY OF MISSING OUT

for the lost

Blessing

A white stag came up
To me and said you'll
Never be an artist,
I said thank you,
Thank you.

Nope / Courtney Love

Diving in a princess dress
Into the
Mosh pit is
Something women do every day
So get up.

I took the last bottle of bubbly and
Walked to the park
I dared some magic to happen

But instead

I saw people's feet
And kites and
Was reminded once more I was nuts
Impossible woman
Better marry while I'm still pretty

Get on the payroll
Or die

S'cool

I'm so heartbroken
WTF am I even looking for
Alone on the stoop
Hungry
Walked a few miles in heels
Cause I couldn't afford
The fare
At 37
But it's OK
I really believe this world that
I'm building
Is cool

Joyride

Skinny dirt road
In the middle of the ocean.
That led to the house of art.
I took it. The engine nearly
Drowned. I lied that it was fun
That I'd do it again. When I got to
That shore
The house was gone and when
I looked back, so was the path.
Now I'm old. Drown in my bed
A thousand miles inland.
For years I thought
I could
Art my way back. Cats sing
Of rose dawns. This country's a
Mirror image
Of the one I left, except
I've bad dreams. And
You're the only
Person who's not here.
Is it the same
For you.

Every Time I Think Nature Can't Shock Me Any More, I Discover Something Like This. Wow.

Remember feelings before emoji

Remember seeing the stars in the sky?

I remember really being alone

Emoji remember feelings to me

Like glitter recalls stars in the sky

And loneliness smells of company

We experience new old feelings with each new emoji

New old stars are discovered every year

And named after their captors—

Emoji sign feelings...

Stars embody an old light!

With the retinal lag of departure...

Come back to me as emoji,

Or a star

That doesn't reach after meaning,

Wow.

No Filter

            wow
so debt   few job
            wow
bad hair   soon die
            no brand
wow
            such life
no time   wow
            pls halp
much love   so real
            amaze
                    wow

Firegram

Like a river of dope
Your love came to me
A superstar—and even if celebrity is
The prostitute sister of love, its economy
Still strikes us both as true,
And so we do do the world's work. We adore.
Stars gossip with a look of love on the world's edge.
The overlooked, broken, the queer and dark—
All those Heathcliffy words
Relax into a
Sphere of unsafety—
Remember 'we were never meant
To survive'—
Her sex *is* the power and like
Literally my dildos have melted
From the heat
Of that fire emoji

Captions for a Cartoon
(comic sans toi)

The machine dispensed
the pill into my sleeping body
and I awoke from the dream of life

I was on a broken ship
caught in the orbit of a long
dead star

how long was I asleep?
I stretched, made my way to
the one-person pod and ejected

out into space. I had to continue my mission

Earth's last fossil, a total heart
wasn't gonna deliver itself
to the fireplace
at the center of space and

as I bobbed along
I forgave you
for waking me

remotely but
every star I pass

makes me think of you

When I return to earth
everyone I know
will be long dead. I'll live alone

in a ruin computerized
to serve me in your voice

No, space is not for pussies

buries face in words

At first I thought these were regular birds.
Then I looked closer, and—
Spurious
Divinity delivery systems
In the veldt w/out God
Where his avatar remains,
The
Most Fought Over Girl On Earth—

omfg
#g_d
<3 <3 <3

Searching…
Searching…

Hope 2 find u,
Sweet celestial
Sadistic_mistress
Nearer 2 me than tachycardia
Or *this* speech,

The rain...
O wow, *the* rain!
Praise b I've got my camera in me.

Eine Kleine

This with you
It's like masturbating at
five years old in a pool of gold
sunlight

Blissful bee
Vertigo train
Snow hinge

The warmth that comes when
outside there's only death.

Diana

If you crossed us you'd get
a diamond snowflake
good for cutting the throats
of stars
to steal their words. It's a wound
that can only be healed
with a strawberry
and so we do, and
disappear
into the funny softness at the deep end of the field

Sender Unknown

This night v. late
I went into the kitchen.
and looked out at
sharp winter stars.
Such a de facto handful
of diamonds and so
I cried a little. Bc
that's your name and
your eye a bit, of diamonds
the back of your teeth,
your past, maybe
even I if I
stared long enough?
a diamond.
So I cried and stayed here on Earth

Which is also a star

Carpe Damn

The screen is raining or
bleeding a bit
of white

The edges of the screen are fuzzy
wuzzy

Am I tired or in love

So calm like everything's forgiven
and
the army goes home forever into

The sunset, the forest,
the rain

And I'm beginning. *Je commence*
the long ascent
out of

The screen—I'm outside!
Omfg. Check it out—

The snow is real

The Night I Fucked William Carlos Williams,

I was alarmed at how stark
his mien was. Everything was 👍 a root

& he: horizon, brutal nekkid little shack—

"Fulfill my destiny as a fisherman—" … The loneliness of Londre, Moscau—

a 1000 Likes or Londons won't save you from "hope

there's something essential at least
to his loneliness." I hoped so. So it was the canon

gave him to me…past I never had…a
pinkness. I had to save him

have him to be, I
turned him to a girl
Bit her pearls and choked on her hair straight till she sang:

"Deli rose, rose of ages:
in the melty shadow and heaves in the torrent of chassis
I exited cardboard snow & entered
the shadow of liberty. A simple winter blooms in
my surfboard, the lyric the lyric of it

was never God, always
'bout the Rose," and fuck if I'll ever risk it for some Majesty again—

Goodbye NJ.
Horizon divided
Horse split in two but
Painlessly

Out of the muffin milk of WCW
came out pure song, the product of her sugar factory,
WCW, exacto metaflower, forgive

me ladybug
for taking on
this form: in my past life
I was a flower, and in the one before that a flower,
and in the one
before a flower.

Or: suddenly, everything's mildness
everything comes roses
I am because my little bitch fucks me—I—

William Carlos Williams
reached their legs up till they looked like arms
and confirmed to me in childhood that
layering's good

Possibly it's everything.

The Coat

If I can, I'd like to
Drag the coat of love off of her
Which I so carefully placed there,
And put it on you—

Or maybe it's already
Slipped off her shoulders and
It would be easy to just
Scoop it up off the floor
And leave

Silently while she

Sits there among the black gleaming apples

Troll Your Soul

The sky doesn't want you to go
The wind doesn't want you to go
Trash cans don't want you to go
Cabs don't want you to go
The book doesn't want you to go
It's not just me

I saw the sky lady
Carry
A small gold center
Like the sky's pistil—
And that was you,
Like the world's baby or something

But at night sometimes the wings
Get dark and cold
Oh darkling can you tell me if
Someone has stepped
On my shadow

I'll Never Forget the Way You Said "Sabine"

Will we marry like
We said or will I become
A less social Greta Garbo.
Today I made sex
Then worked all day in
Affordable housing
Worked like a sub then
Loved like one.
Why am I so poor
And old. It's so cold my
Fingers have grown new
Lace. I want it to be spring
I want
A thousand a flowers to bloom,
Let's pretend that "a" wasn't there,
But see, I never felt
So free, so I
Put perfume on my soles
(I really do) and
Sleep

Sent Remotely

You love me only with
A veil, a bride, or
Through a barrier, screen or when
I'm on a trip
Somewhere green away
I can't
Afford to travel
So I go into people's
Arms to write
You postcards
Maybe when I'm dead
You'll love me the most
It will be like I'm always traveling

The Night I Almost Fucked Ezra Pound

Black square of the hair of Ezra Pound—
Let them find me having choked on it
She says No

A 1000x No and
I die a bit at the opera—

Later she travels
I text her my distressed torso she'll receive only
When back from the undergrounds of patina

Of course I'd make her sausage
She'll only eat things made from my flesh
And sooner die big than

A little
In the motel Edge of Sliver
Back in 68 I told her

Watch me while I do it to myself and
Tell me you prefer others. That I'm nothing. Instead

She reached and unspooled a wheel
Of flesh
Croatia, Serbia, Gorgona

And when I came I never knew
Whom I was coming for to cry

The 1% of me that's utile
Wants to serve her
With the versatility of the title
In a silent film and as
Robert Houdin pulls the skeleton from Woman, she
Pulled use out of me

Pure purée of poetry
The day in which the sun
Of poem will make everything clear

Shine on me, your jet face
Shine on me my victim
In a dawn the memorial
Faraway marble
The same old nuclear landscape at the edge of Leave

If this is not the lyric then
What is

The thing you kill, though

Nothing could be fairer and clearer
Than a trailer with two hearts painted on it
Sitting in the middle of the ocean

The murder of civilians or
The sound of music.

Where is the word in which I might
just sit by you and eat?

Star Words

You're in your world now
and you're happy.
To fuck your brains out
through your eyes? Nah, dying.
End poem. I don't even want to see the sunset
Anymore.

Wait... NOW: you're mad
With what you know, everyone leaves
The way they've left me: now will you take
This ugly-ass flower
I hand over—
Take it.

Bless your family
And the day you were born
And the salt that feathered
The shore
Of neue Eu
Who needs a pronoun

Since you

#Endpoem.

Buffalo

Perfect girls singing
In liberated silos

The industrial revolution didn't
Save us nor will the digital

Is what I'm thinking as I see
On the one basic

Inner channel
Us walking high and happy in the snow

Of this immemorial year
I loved you and still do

What do you think, who will be
The last to text before

One of us dies
I get that you didn't want to wake up

Each morning to a mental goddess
But I really did trust

You n I would make it
I'll be so mad

If love turns out not to be a person

Airquote

No one but
The state and god
Will watch you high and crying at 4:45am

My two cats
God and the State
I was happy for the attention
Though I could have also used
A hug—

No, Emptiness, not you.
I'm not that desperate.

As if.
You wish.
Do you picture me like this
During your
Unimaginable masturbation,
Carriage ride through the green, what you

Communicate to me
Not even through loss but these
New things I find, same and same,

"Always been such a lonely child,"

"In the town I grew up there were many wells,"

I can't even remember
Starting writing this,
I can't even

And will I ever
See Europe again and why

Afterparty

I threw a party
But I didn't invite my lovers
So that I could be free
In the morning
At the window
The tree me and
The mirror
It's all I need
A frame a subject
A mode of production
And someone to talk to
Who is me

Con Mucho Ánimo

Since I detourned love
I find I'm (tho I've tried to go into like,
Solitude) embracing people
To whom I turn
Con ánimo alegre,
Who are as fucked as I am
As free as me
It's neat
Let's suffer the great glacier together
Let us surround ourselves with
Stupid pleasures

Secretly

kid trips in his room
bangs his head on the desk
gets up

the dog climbs on the bed and
thrashes around in ecstasy

you open the computer, check the
new photos she was tagged in

a drone alights

who's picking their nose even as we
speak amirite

and everyone masturbates

in bed when he wakes, he compares
her body to Susan's

Susan flirts with the girl at the gym

really running is her special time to
space out to swelling bass and think
of this guy who killed himself over her

only that never happened

it's from "The Dead"

we wipe away tears of regret

kid hides 7/11 coffee in a
Starbucks cup

at dawn they collect the bottles and
cans

now the dude tries on his dead
wife's clothes

people have amazing online lives

a cancer begins

Rayan wakes up in the basement to
a banging noise

she's terrified and chained

the sky above the mountaintop turns
hazy orange

an idea about a newspaper called
Secretly

appears to me in a dream:

right, my dreams kept escaping so I
set up a camera to find out why

when I play the film back, it's a still
of a mountaintop

above a sign hangs in sans serif

I just repeat what it says.

Afterbirth

I wasn't me with them
I was mad with them
Bc they loved my body only
Inside the institution
& I didn't want that cash

Fuck you
For not loving me for
I was "crazy"
And wouldn't "get a job"
Trying to love your lazy

Socialized ass was job enough
Run from the institutions
Run from your lovers
Run from currency
To the current

ocean

LOL

Life is lol
Love is lol
Pain is lol
The wind is lol
Cats are lol
Dreams are lol
You are awake
When all is lol

Song

People are
Getting jobs
Getting married and moving
Away I'm still here
Alone like neon
Admiring the moon
In the puddle of a penknife

No wife
No child
Just seed and a will
To reflect and when sun
Drops behind the Brooklyn roofs
I'm in colors too.

Awoke. Again

I wrote you a
Short story about a man who
Was dating a voice-over artist whose
Voice was the voice
Of subway announcements, so every time
He took the train he basked in her
And when they broke up it was
A swansong terrible
Terrible

I'm writing you a
Dreamer-for-hire ad: Too scared
To dream? I'll dream your dreams
For you, cheap nightly rates!
"Because they're your dreams,
I'm just having them!"

I
I write you a poem
Is it really so terrible to be alone
Would it be so bad to be
A junkie dominatrix
High off her voice in the evening choir
In this light even
My name seems mysterious to me,

Is yours mysterious to you?
Who's having all these loves

Who thinks only about sex and race,
Who doubts
Own reason when
Hemmed in by white lies
Like butterflies... Who's talking the talk

Who's walking in your dream?

#JeSuisCVS

My brain is falling apart
So I'm allowed to talk.

"Turn around and sleep my love
And I'll hold you" I actually

Said this to a body
On this planet where
There are such things as forks

And gods, and police cars on fire.
My goal in life

Is to be a traitor to my race.
I don't want things anymore

You've made me hate on them. When
You got yr bottle service
On the mine fields
Of Instagram and drowned

In silky lagunas
In filters–
Promoting your own death!

The revolutionary potential
I felt in you is gone

Now you're just a
Banana peel framed

Solicitously
In the museum of the desert

No Regrets

I can't be in your exhibition
Because I won't hurt what I love

Despite the discourse despite
Nuance I can't deny
A single tear

I can't be in your exhibition because
Stars

Can't accept the position
In the academy of hate
Held in
Dark woods where
You think you'll be safe if you bow to
Daddy but you won't

Keep the cv and the champagne
Take a pill or something,
I'm out

Love Song of Social Defeat

Maybe it's true I'm crazy
And you're a wonderful person
But I did have the bruises
I asked for
In my snowflake voice
As we fought the system
Wildly
On through each other's bodies
Dust & lust
Are beautiful

But the greatest of these
Is hope
For a deep trove true love
Crying sculpture
Burning car
I'd rather be
A mad nun than snooze in the
Market of senses
That's how you and I
Are different

In your way
You love the world and
I love in mine
I'd have loved to have been
Your doll but I'm on fire
With crescents and tails of stars
And don't want to shop or
Spend in restaurants

I wanted the cash
To end

Perfect Post

Tonight I could write
The perfect post
That each of the people I had loved
Would Like
Then would I know that
All is forgiven
Since we're gone so soon
We're like the summer

Star Rain

I don't want to die in your cell
Said Ralkina Jones
I have nothing to say
Except that I'm with you
And love you
And will fight when you say
We should all get to die under the sky

You Are an Epitome of Beauty

I thought of a marvelous
Trick:
If you're reading this
And having negative
Thoughts imagine
Now those thoughts
Exiting through
Your shoulder blades—
As soon as they hit the air
They're seahorses
Behind your back they're
Building an air school to
Hash it all out. Now
Picture the seahorses
Coming to show you
The results of
Their long studies
They say we are too pretty
To be sad
And the deep
Inside you though dark
Is full of
Electric coral—
We only got negative
Because we couldn't
Be seen but now
We can see our beauty
Now we're educated
Let us teach you!

Then they show you joy.

Promise

I'm leaving this for you
Tonight
When in distraction and
Loneliness you
Turn to social media
For a signal or
Symbol
This is it!
... It's ok
I promise
Go to sleep I'll be here.

Tonight I am reborn
As Happy Ghost
You can contact me
Via Ouija, baby
I'm the Weegee
Of passion crimes committed
Solely in the mountains of
Mind
Where streams flow
Whose water
Marbles like flesh and where
Werewhos prey...
Rise into the tree crowns,
Star of day
Be the monster whose each step
Makes wood blooms
Forever verb.

Santa Mania

Mania my sweetest nectar
Don't leave me
I was walking in the sun

Listening to Lana I was here
Before my birth and
Here I remain
Dreaming intensely with
Great plans to live and die

Do I really have to?
I guess it doesn't mattress

I'm here and I like
To fuck.

Symptoms

I started writing down
My symptoms but
They were such boring words
Like, fake. So then I thought
I'd turn my mind to objects;
What could be realer, right? —
Hello bureau
Hello vanity
Hello bedside table
Hello bed
With the girl in it with lifted feet
(not me btw). Saying this
With my mind I got braver and
Looked out the window
(the OG browser)
Outside was outside
The building next door held many
Opportunities to ponder
The fates of other men
And women, both cis and trans
And objects
But nah, I was tired
I'm tired
This is happening now
I'm walking across the room
To get another smoke
What happens next
Will astonish you

Busted Xmas Card

I'm writing a novel
(I think) in which
the things that in this century
are called bipolar
immigrant lesbian
are actual superpowers
Raise your crazy hand if you've imagined
how in another time
you'd be a witch a shaman! or just
another migrant locked up & labored into fine mist
And it's now about that time
Xtians celebrate
the birth of boy wonder
whose trip they dig but
can't quite follow, all over
they're mounting stars on barbed wire
Wow even I bought something
off amazon
a guy earning $12/hr packed it
another walked in the cold
to deliver
identical plastic gold toy trains
to a family tossed by isms straight up war and the art world
And no one was indicted in the prison murder of
#sayhername
There's still time for a ride
to the mall or an endtimesy
orgy between friends
dope or daime
before the ball drops
I don't pretend
to understand what goes on

around me
that's my superpower
I don't mind
your gaze from a distance
Who wants to hold the hand anyway
of a damaged refugee liar
Who struggles with you
a great spotted beast in inverted dioramas
where there's such a thing
as the death of the market
and difference and love
are key
They're fucking key

Hot Rubber Whores

I started writing
how being learnéd was OK, but also being
simple, that I loved both, when I got
the cancer of the pancreas and
died. That's all. Now, in my next life
I'm a drop of sweat between the mask
and cheek of a protester.
But since thought is already
half deed, I'm also halfway
to the farm where my ex grandpa
opens the door for me, turns on
the radio. We sit. Just then,
just past the border of New Jersey, the night
turns he, moon a she.
I've been asleep for centuries, who
wakes me now?

It Took So Long for the War to Catch Up

When art eats love,
Then what?
I've seen a beautiful home shine by the riverbank.
And I saw the hut of murder.
That's where I went in.
My grandfather
Cleared the farm for you—
Fields in the distance and frost,
And gave you grandma's dress.
Stitched roses on white.
The marionettes hung free.
He was the only man I loved.
Was he lying to me? Instead of
To the farm, the humility of life
I went to death, what was unwanted.
To go to perish alone.
Two bloods
Two wounds
Two wives.
I beg forgiveness of the fields:
They were but I
Never was a real blonde.

Buffet of Air

I was fixing to sing a poem about
the multiverse so green, the stars
just fanning away from each other—
I couldn't hack it. Chipped my tooth &
ran away. In the form of a Llhasa Apso
called Poldie, I wandered
the city streets, listening to what the people
were saying. I really wanted
to chime in. In time the impulse
faded. Maybe the new revolt is
not to reveal a damn thing.

Clouds

So what kind of art
Are you making
These days—
You into currency,
Almanacs,
Colorlessness...?

— No—indexology.

Then she walked away

Stormy Bodies

I achieved notoriety
Through my blog
Dead Birds of Instagram
And then I ascended to heaven and
Was seated
At the right hand of the mother
Of sadness
Called Sunday
Her eyes were tall.

Baroque

Here's the great Tumblrer, they whispered as
he walked by in robes of naked dragon gold.
Tumblrer, Tumblrer they chanted when they
burnt the rotting books in pyres the Woman
stepped out of. Tumble!
It's not the joy I give you, not travel but
winterface, interlocking vines that could go
this way sans end, and they do.
Scroll. Scroll.
The dawn is breaking, war is starting, you're
my magician forever.
I cried when you left me for a critic
in the provinces.
Oh for those sleigh bells! And Lisztmas is
coming—its mania
a brooch that shades
the me and the other...
Sleep. Sleep.
A cameo cradles
the thumbnail of your changing profile
in Heaven.

TIJTS

I'm sorry I have eaten
Mixed nuts
That were in my coat pocket
I'm falling asleep

In an empty gallery
Literally no one
Cares
That I ate the nuts

Viral

I should know.
I keep a shadow
Twitter for my depression
Where I blurb all the terrible things
I think and do not do
Because it's all about not doing
I cry when I'm pretty
Feelings are like filters
Depression's like love
You'll know her when you see her face

Deperson

My scholarship
Remote as a cloud
Sown with mines
Sewn in like buttons on a couch
Doesn't talk to me
Like my last lover
Like I don't even exist so I
Show them—
I don't and
With great care
The landlord's son
Plants a little pink blue flag in the front yard sun

2 Worlds

It doesn't matter if I feel loved
Maybe I can't and it doesn't

Matter if anyone
Gets a thing I say

All that matters is I should stay
And die only when it's time

But what if it's time.
In another world they're singing

My songs off of cereal boxes
In this one I'm alone

Sky Jesus

I bought a 13 inch
statue of Jesus
made of wood and resin and I
spraypainted &
decaled clouds on it.

It's called Sky Jesus

The act was supposed to
magically free him
from having to suffer
from expression

I made him

and still it's night and
you're not here

Where's my drugs

Dispatches from the West

An eye
Needled in an experiment
Turns into reptile eye
Then a planet
Every day I'm less human
Is that because the older I get
I get more like the stars I'm made of
I fired my bodyguards
I'm tall enough to die

Elegy Sonata

Weep 4 Vladimir, for he is dead,
in his youthful skin
a halo departing from his body,

He's gone to where he can always chainsmoke
and feel just fine and drink
and run in the meadows
ko mladi pas,

Wish I could say you were
like a father to me;
still tho I remember
the white bedcurtains of the mental *ospedale*

Like a pedal
something efficient
that turned you to a ghost
surrounded at the kitchen table by the family

I'm high as fuck and listening to
the song of the earth
recordings from space and I wonder
if I can hear you in there somewhere Vlado,

You died on your birthday
we hope you had fun, your epitaph:
"So what's up?" forever carried by the nimbus chorus
by ruthless crystals

By fucking angels.

---

ko mladi pas = like a young dog

Endless Weather

Approach a window
In my hand and look out:
A lake going thru somewhere.
Yeah lake.
Put on a show for me baby.
Sometimes the deep greenness
Comes visit me, sometimes it pulls back.
Tha greenness. This greenie
Memory fur... tide of affect
That's meaning
Says
My death was a hoax
A kinda star &
I only want to talk about the weather,
Tits blowing in the wind.
When I'm deported
Leave a rose a few months in a row
In what used to be my mailbox,
Then flake out. I'll be
Hiding inside flowers
In almost nothing ;)

Almond Breeze Contains No Almonds

I'm the lonely cornholio
Literally I'm flayed
By what I become into
A casualty
Of raw
Petals
On the periphery of function
A lost little domme
Hits on me tonight
I bring her home and
Put her to bed & now
Next to her I'm dreaming
Of oppressive circus rooms
Parrying the sallies of great cats
Being raped by a
Laughing sadist
On top of the IMAGINE sign
Or what's more painful
Of an alternate universe
I pray to wake into
For good
Where I'm all me and
You love me
While here
The only thing I'm still made of is you

Locus Solus

I remember as when we trusted each other
We had the possibility of a tree
It was neat to vibe like a newly discovered god
Whose places of service
Had not been imagined yet
But we tried
We said disco wood
Friend bonfires
And it was easy to spot them in the night summer air
That gathered like the perfect soundtrack
I still hear
Piped in from a small wound
In the side of my mountain
When I'm happy I know I'm in a poem

Fall's Like

Bladder pressure is like
Coming is like crying
Like trying to pass
A stone through your eye
This would be a good night
For love and drugs
But instead I'm here
In my nude mind and so
Become the priestess
Crossing my fingers I
Get kidnapped
Into the sex trade and
Suffer crossing the sierras
In the prison
A bird of one color
Comes to the window
In my chest
Like spring

Super Maria

Only my death would save
My brand at this point
But I'm fighting

For a reason to stay
And always I go back to the

Sign
Fragrant
"Like the summer"

Lecture

Poets...have always...
I'm falling asleep...

Livethinking

Before I came out here
I thought I must be going
Soon
And then I looked at the stars
Now maybe even the seasons have
changed.
I'm still out here

This bark I hear will last forever.

Like

When I die
Who will try to figure out
The last thing that
I Liked
Anyone?
The last song I played
Who cares
I will go on like
The jewel from the Titanic
In deepest darkest depths
Till something grows
Out of me
And I become coral
Inhabited by millions
Of song

Suicide Power Ballad

To keep it super brite
Even tho' you too cray may be for anyone,
Shine that shine then tears
In face and in paper
Sometimes I think wow
Sivvy was so young when she went and sometimes
I'm amazed
& proud of her for holding out so long
Through Chantal's taped solitudes,
Duration can also be solace if you wait
Long enough for the tears
To stop
And her planets come out in briteness into the empty living room

Sometimes they don't,
You get on the totallypackedtrain
In mirror shades
Dexedrine
Cry brown thoughts and later reapply
The colors like such the good ghost…
Dream this feel is gone but sure enough it waits
For us to wake up
A kinda cat
Then lies on top
And purrs, baby
I'm amazed at the ways you don't love me

In the dream the philosopher
Asked what I was even about & I said
La connaissance de là-bas,
I'm writing this cause if I die tonight
I don't want the last thing I typed
To be a porn search,
Instead I want to say
Love you and now the body's
Out of the picture
I'm the ideal girl for you

And I'm setting out
On the long ice to where the other brave girls went
The site of the thought that knows
Even though
I'm the only one who can save me from sadness,
I wish
It would've been you
But now it's not. The thought crashed back in
And took me out to see
The perfect chords

Migration

I never want to get any
More new things.
I wanna wear out these shoes white
And walk on the rug till it's perfectly
Colorless
To wear the shoes dark
Walking on an abyss that's been worn out
The shoes carry me,
I can't help it,
I fly above the desert with no name

Ugh

I don't even care anymore.
Watch me not
Care
Wasted, high
Blind blonde
Moth is just a loser butterfly
That picks fake
Suns
Over a flower

Laterz

You got me where
You want me
A shiny memory a curse
To pray to, whatever
I'm immaterial
So I sleep many hours, pull up
In a fly hearse to
The House of Death
A tall black square I'm 'sposed
To tremble before, I take a pic
And put it on Instagram
Outside, the porch
Runs into the shallows
Where a preacher melts into
The surf, reborn
As a foam idea
And inside
Trees make their own wild
Arrangements in the
Dining room nook
I hide in the bathroom
To masturbate
When I come out it's summer
Our kid is playing
On the veranda
Whole house is white
If this is the other world
I'm ready

Reveries

Tonight people are home alone
Watching a show
About androids slowly becoming conscious
Once they can no longer
Escape
The memory of the trauma
Of the West

I feel safest in the morning
As though nothing terrible
Could happen to me in the early sunshine
It's a time for good intentions
And traditionally also
The hour of executions
And surgeries
A good time to set off on a trip

Or be torn from limb to limb
By four sleek deathyard horses
Literally to
Lose your head
When you look at the pillow next to you
Whose head should be there
That once simply just was there
Unquestionably
Like sunlight and now

Reachable only through increasingly virtual methods
I am thinking of timetravel
Of having an android built
That looks and acts
Just like her
It would do the thing with the mouth
And that wish in itself is rape
Cause love, Western love is rape
And so I have to stop loving her like that
I'm fucking trying

Space Is Such a Burden

I was raped
Murdered
But not before I sent you the manuscript
For *Joy of Missing Out*
Or JOMO
The title I promised
To some beautiful children years ago
And the storybook
I showed you
Star of Day
Little girl running
Out into a meadow in the night sun
Walking the mountain
Path once more
What I want to be
My final scene
Shown abstractly on the book's cover—

Epitaph

Here is my last fuck—
I give it to you,
Take it from me

F

The Best Text Message Poem in the World

As you read this, you realize you love me, but I'm dead.

<3

And even now
Even in the (I can't
Believe I'm saying
It) the Trump
Economy (not believing
Is my privilege) the greatest
Hurt is seeing
The back of someone
Who looks like you at the bar
Jet hair trans skin
But it's ok
This pain is how
I know
That love will win

Art History

Some say the night fell like an empire
Some rodeo rider
The neverending time before the deli opens

Let me reincarnate into a deli cat
Or subway rat let me never leave this place
And see my country again

Could've milked my
Sleep for cash
In the window the birds chirp

Same as in the porn I'm watching
The universe frotting and edging
Against nothing

To live alone
Woken by cars fucking
And listen to the microwave winds

Tears a blazin
And so very happy
Haven't gone to sleep since last I was happy

So technically it's still
Same old night we met
The crispy one I was born

Back when we were dinosaur and wore
Water of the Mountain
I didn't have pussy yet

Just a wooden hole for sounds

Women, Weed and Whiskey

I stole my <3 from
the witch

And gave it to this
man-girl but her hands were

Busy holding baggies of
dandelion fluff so

She dropped it and
I handed it to my friend

His girlfriend hates cats
she said Shoo!

And kicked it
I took the <3 to a

Beautiful birdhouse
on a rainy Monday up the mountain

Where a good bird gave it
a really good mic

We sang in the grass pretty much
night and night

To the lovers and
the unlonely dead

For the first time in years I placed
my <3 back in &

Quickly it tunneled deeper
till all I could see was

Its glad path

H.D.

Intermittent sirens
Buzzing
People talking in the walls
Car whoosh
And behind those the sound
Of the greatest loneliness
Ever—

What are these,
Visions. It's really seeing clearly
There must be
Some reason why we're that
Divided—

I keep thinking like I gotta
Go back to
Something, rejoin
The us in some future kingdom,
In the olive groves—

There's also the wind—
The card said he (wind) was also
Me, that I was changing
Something by changing,
So I never did get that
Tattoo of <3

Sorry Anthony Bourdain

Like a Player

The muse is my muse now
Sweet consciousness
Deep pussy image
Don't need you to read her
By the light I can totally taste
Revolving so fast she's still
Like the ground
Dancing summer
Cloud on the deep blue screen of
Death,
I'm not scared anymore.

Joy of Missing Out

I put my fingers
To the little window
And close my eyes
I can text without seeing
Face without touching
Live in a separate stream
Of time
Divided from you
By a shining membrane
That shows me the news
Of shit hitting the fan
And football scores

Somewhere
In that moving cloud
Is a door
I will pass through at death
The moment I'm finally fully
Uploaded into your memory
Don't groan cos I'm
So obsessed with dying
When the door is cracked open
The light
Shines through
The color of tea

I glimpse that moment when
I will be
Forever the one
More absent
Forever the less desiring
And will have paid
The price of flesh
For the total randomness
Of my failures here on earth
Guided but not explained
By the light
Of an unsubstanced star

And I shake my ass

ACKNOWLEDGEMENTS

Warm thanks to the editors who gave some of these poems homes at *About Place Journal, Academy of American Poets, Ampersand Review, BathHouse, Beecher's Magazine, BOMB, Brooklyn Poets Anthology, February: an anthology, Gestalt, Hyperallergic, Imperial Matters, Jubilat, PACKET, Parallax, Pleiades, Poetry Society of America, Prelude, Public Pool, Secret Behavior,* and *Washington Square.*

The quote in "Firegram" is from "A Litany for Survival" by Audre Lorde. "Perfect Post" is after "Tonight I Can Write the Saddest Lines" by Pablo Neruda. "TIJTS" is after "This Is Just To Say" by William Carlos Williams.

Thank you Birds & friends who made *JOMO* a thing, especially Dan Boehl and Eric Amling. Love to Sampson Starkweather, BFF, endless editor and lifesaver. <3 to Miran, Vanda and Viktor Božičević, Kerry Carnahan, Tamara Gruber, and Dia Felix. TY 2 the crew who decided *JOMO* was the best title for this book while I went to the WC at Harlekin Bar in Berlin one long ago day. *JOMO* is in memory of Vladimir Božičević and for everyone who sees a different world.

Ana Božičević, born in Croatia in 1977, is a poet, translator, teacher, and occasional singer. She is the author of *Joy of Missing Out* (Birds, LLC, 2017), the Lambda Award-winning *Rise in the Fall* (Birds, LLC, 2013) and *Stars of the Night Commute* (Tarpaulin Sky Press, 2009). She is the recipient of the 40 Under 40: The Future of Feminism award from the Feminist Press, and the PEN American Center/NYSCA grant for translating *It Was Easy to Set the Snow on Fire* by Zvonko Karanović (Phoneme Media, 2017). At the PhD Program in English at The Graduate Center of the City University of New York she studied New American poetics and alternative art schools and communities, and edited lectures by Diane di Prima for *Lost & Found: The CUNY Poetics Document Initiative*. Ana has read, taught and performed at Art Basel, Bowery Poetry Club, Harvard, Naropa University, San Francisco State University Poetry Center, the Sorbonne, Third Man Records, University of Arizona Poetry Center, and The Watermill Center. She works and teaches poetry at BHQFU, New York's freest art school.